THE ONLY TRIVIA BOOK YOU'LL EVER NEED

THE MOST RANDOM, CRAZY, FUNNY & STRANGE FACTS FOR A CURIOUS MIND - GUARANTEED TO CURE BOREDOM

JOE MURPHY

AT PUBLISHING

Joe Murphy

indirect, which are incurred as a result of the use of the information contained within this document, including, but not limited to, — errors, omissions, or inaccuracies.

The Only Trivia Book You'll Ever Need: First Edition

If you LOVE knowing *uncomfortably random facts...*

This book is for YOU!

F*ck an introduction, let's just get straight into it.

THE ACTOR VERNE TROYER WHO PLAYS MINI-ME IN AUSTIN POWERS HAD TO DO ALL HIS OWN STUNTS DUE TO HIS SIZE.

A TEENAGER IN TAIWAN DIED AFTER PLAYING THE VIDEO GAME *DIABLO 3*. THE TEENAGER PLAYED THE GAMES FOR 40 HOURS STRAIGHT WITHOUT EATING A THING...*NO COMMENT*.

AMERICA HAS THE MOST AMOUNT OF NUCLEAR AIRCRAFT CARRIERS WITH A TOTAL OF 11, EACH ONE HOSTING 80 FIGHTER JETS. IN ADDITION TO THIS, THE TOTAL AMOUNT OF DECK SPACE ON THEM, ARE LARGER THAN THE ENTIRE WORLD'S NUCLEAR AIRCRAFT CARRIERS COMBINED.

IN 2012, THE FINANCE MINISTER OF ZIMBABWE MADE AN ANNOUNCEMENT TO THE WORLD EXCLAIMING THAT THE NATION HAD 217 DOLLARS IN THE BANK. *THE COUNTRY MUST HAVE BEEN BROKE BROKE.*

A WOMAN CALLED PENNY BROWN SAVED A YOUNG MAN'S LIFE CALLED KEVIN STEPHAN BY GIVING HIM CPR AFTER HE WAS HIT BY A BASEBALL BAT. SEVEN YEARS AFTER THE INCIDENT, STEPHAN WOULD REPAY THE FAVOUR AND GO ON TO SAVE PENNY'S LIFE BY PERFORMING THE HEIMLICH MANOEUVRE AFTER SHE BEGAN CHOKING ON FOOD. *WELL, YOU GET WHAT YOU GIVE...*

IRON MAN WAS CREATED BY STAN LEE IN 1963, AT THE PEAK OF THE COLD WAR. STAN WANTED TO MAKE A CHARACTER PEOPLE WOULD HATE AND YET STILL GET TO A POINT WHERE THEY WOULD LIKE HIM. *R.I.P STAN LEE.*

MEN WHO ARE UNHAPPILY MARRIED ARE HAPPIER WITH THEIR LIVES IF THEIR WIVES ARE SATISFIED WITH THEIR MARRIAGES.

THE FIRST PRESIDENT TO LIVE IN THE WHITE HOUSE IS JOHN ADAMS AND THE ONLY PRESIDENT WHO DIDN'T LIVE IN THE WHITE HOUSE WAS GEORGE WASHINGTON.

IN 1886, KARL BENZ AND EMILE LEVASSOR INVENTED THE FIRST WORKING AND OPERATING AUTOMOBILE.

WOMEN EQUALITY WAS SO BAD IN THE 1900S THAT WOMEN WERE NOT ALLOWED TO SMOKE IN PUBLIC. KATIE MULCAHY WAS A YOUNG WOMAN WHO LIVED IN NEW YORK AND WAS ARRESTED AFTER LIGHTING A MATCH AND ATTEMPTING TO SMOKE A CIGARETTE. AFTER ARGUING HER CASE IN COURT, SHE WAS FINED $5.

THE CENTENNIAL LIGHT BULB IS MAINTAINED BY THE LIVERMORE-PLEASANTON FIRE DEPARTMENT. THE FIRE DEPARTMENT CLAIMS THAT THE BULB IS AT LEAST 119 YEARS OLD (INSTALLED IN 1901) AND HAS ONLY BEEN TURNED OFF A HANDFUL OF TIMES. THIS MAKES THE CENTENNIAL LIGHT BULB THE LONGEST LASTING LIGHT BULB IN THE WORLD.

A YOUNG TEEN WHO WENT BY THE NAME BOY JONES WAS CAUGHT BREAKING INTO BUCKINGHAM PALACE AND STEALING QUEEN VICTORIA'S UNDER PANTS. *NOW THAT'S A PERVY TEEN.*

THE WORLD'S OLDEST PARLIAMENT IS LOCATED IN ICELAND. THE PARLIAMENT HAS BEEN ABOUT SINCE 930.

IN MEDIEVAL IRELAND, MURDERERS WOULD BE GIVEN TO DISEASED FAMILIES AS SLAVES IF THEY DIDN'T PAY THEIR FINE. AT THIS POINT THE FAMILY HAD THE MURDERERS AS A BELONGING AND COULD KILL THEM IF THEY CHOSE TO. *IF ONLY THIS LAW WAS STILL INTACT.*

KFC SUED THE COLONEL FOR $120 MILLION AFTER HE ANNOUNCED PLANS TO OPEN A RESTAURANT CALLED 'CLAUDIA SANDERS, THE COLONEL'S LADY'. DURING HIS LIFETIME, THE MAN BEHIND THE POULTRY OPENED UP A COMPETING FRIED-CHICKEN RESTAURANT BECAUSE HE DESPISED WHAT KENTUCKY FRIED CHICKEN HAD BECOME.

INDIA IS RESPONSIBLE FOR ROUGHLY 75% OF THE WORLD'S DISTRIBUTION OF SPICES.

HIPPOS LOVE TO LICK CROCODILES. DUE TO THE FACT THE HIPPOS AREN'T A THREAT TO THE CROCS, THEY TOLERATE IT. *NOW THAT'S WHAT YOU CALL FRIENDSHIP.*

ROUGHLY 381 KILOGRAMS OF WHITE SAND WASHES UP IN HAWAII. THIS WHITE SAND IS PREDOMINANTLY MADE UP OF LARGE PARROTFISII POOP.

SLOTHS ARE THE WORLD'S SLOWEST ANIMAL ON LAND, BUT ARE THREE TIMES FASTER IN WATER. THEY CAN HOLD THEIR BREATHS UPWARDS OF 40 MINUTES AT A TIME!

MIKE TYSON IS ARGUABLY ONE OF THE GREATEST HEAVYWEIGHT BOXERS OF ALL TIME. AS A TEEN, HE WAS ARRESTED AN UNBELIEVABLE AMOUNT OF TIMES... APPROXIMATELY 38 BEFORE THE AGE OF... HAVE A GUESS...13. HE EVENTUALLY GOT HIMSELF OFF THE STREETS AS HE FOUND BOXING AND WELL, THE REST IS HISTORY. *IRON MIKE, WHAT A COME-UP STORY.*

RAVENS ARE ONE OF THE SMARTEST ANIMALS ON EARTH. IF A RAVEN KNOWS ANOTHER RAVEN IS WATCHING, IT HIDES ITS FOOD. IT WILL PRETEND TO PUT THE FOOD IN ONE PLACE WHILE REALLY HIDING IT IN ANOTHER. *I NEED TO START DOING THIS TO MY SIBLINGS*.

THE INTERNET, YOUR BRAIN AND THE UNIVERSE SHARE THE SAME GROWTH DYNAMICS AND NETWORKING SYSTEMS PATTERNS. *AWESOME…*

THE BEATLES NEVER STOOD FOR ANY FORM OF DISCRIMINATION. THEY OFTEN REFUSED TO PLAY AT ANY CLUBS WHICH WERE SEGREGATED. THEY TRULY BELIEVED IN RACIAL EQUALITY.

MAKE SURE YOU GET YOUR SLEEP. SO MANY DISASTERS HAPPEN DUE TO PEOPLE FALLING ASLEEP WHILST ON IMPORTANT JOBS. TO NAME A FEW DISASTERS: CHERNOBYL, THE THREE MILE ISLAND ACCIDENT AND THE SPACE SHUTTLE CHALLENGER DISASTER.

WHAT IS 111,111,111 X 111,111,111? 12345678987654321. *WELL, THAT'S JUST BEAUTIFUL.*

THERE IS A GIANT TORTOISE CALLED JONATHAN WHO LIVES ON THE ISLAND ST HELENA IN THE SOUTH PACIFIC OCEAN. JONATHAN WAS BORN IN 1832 AND IS STILL ALIVE TODAY, MAKING HIM THE LONGEST LIVING ANIMAL ON EARTH AT A WHOPPING 188 YEARS OLD. *AND THEY SAY IMMORTALITY ISN'T A THING, WELL TELL THAT TO MY FRIEND JONNY.*

THE LONGEST YEAR IN HUMAN HISTORY WAS IN 46 BC, CONTAINING 445 DAYS.

MOST PEOPLE THINK THEY HATE WORK, UNTIL THEY FIND OUT THAT THERE ARE PEOPLE WHO ACTUALLY HAVE A PHOBIA OF WORK - IT'S CALLED 'ERGOPHOBIA'.

THE FIRST MAN TO EVER SWIM THE ENTIRE LENGTH OF GREAT BRITAIN WAS A MAN CALLED SEAN CONWAY. THE TOTAL LENGTH OF THE SWIM WAS 900 MILES WHICH TOOK HIM 135 DAYS. 90 OF WHICH WERE SPENT IN THE WATER AND THE REST, WELL... RESTING. *PRETTY IMPRESSIVE, RIGHT?*

JUST LIKE WE MOURN THE DEATH OF OUR LOVED ONES, SO DO ELEPHANTS. THIS PROCESS CAN SOMETIMES LAST YEARS.

COMPETITORS FROM ALL OVER THE WORLD COME TOGETHER AND ARE GIVEN 5 MINUTES TO TELL THE BIGGEST LIE THEY CAN THINK OF. BY DOING SO, THEY CAN WIN THE WORLD'S BIGGEST LIAR COMPETITION. THIS COMPETITION IS HELD ANNUALLY IN THE UK. *MY EX-GIRLFRIEND WOULD HAVE WON THAT EASILY. I FORGOT TO MENTION THAT FUNNILY ENOUGH, POLITICIANS ARE BANNED FROM THIS TOURNAMENT.*

IN 1860 ABRAHAM LINCOLN STARTED TO GROW HIS BEARD AS HE GOT A LETTER FROM A YOUNG WOMAN CALLED GRACE BETEL. THE LETTER SAID IF HE GREW HIS BEARD, SHE WOULD CONVINCE HER HUSBAND TO VOTE FOR HIM.

IN PSYCHOLOGY, THE TERM 'RECIPROCAL LIKING' IS USED TO DESCRIBE THE PHENOMENON THAT OCCURS WHEN YOU START LIKING PEOPLE BECAUSE THEY LIKE YOU. THIS OCCURS BECAUSE WE LIKE TO SURROUND OURSELVES WITH PEOPLE WHO MAKE US FEEL GOOD.

IN FINLAND THERE IS A WIFE-CARRYING CONTEST HELD ANNUALLY. THE MEN HAVE TO GIVE THEIR SPOUSE A PIGGYBACK WHILST HAVING A RACE EACH OTHER. THE WINNING COUPLE RECEIVES THEIR WIFE'S WEIGHT IN BEER.

PABLO ESCOBAR WAS THE MOST INFAMOUS DRUG DEALER OF ALL TIME; AT HIS PEAK HE HAD AN ESTIMATED NET WORTH OF 30 BILLION. PABLO ESCOBAR WAS MAKING ROUGHLY 600 MILLION PER WEEK THROUGH THE SALES OF COCAINE. HE HAD SO MUCH MONEY THAT HE OFFERED TO PAY OFF COLOMBIA'S DEBT IF THEY STOPPED TRACKING HIM. *THAT IS A PROFOUND AMOUNT OF MONEY.*

AS PART OF A FUNDRAISER, BRAZILIAN ADELIR ANTÔNIO DE CARLI TIED TIED 1,000 BALLOONS TO AN ARMCHAIR SO HE COULD TRY AND BREAK THE WORLD RECORD FOR THE LONGEST TIME SPENT IN THE AIR WITH BALLOONS. ALTHOUGH THIS WAS A FUNDRAISER AND A GOOD GESTURE, IT'S A PRETTY STUPID ONE. THE WIND TOOK HIM OFF COURSE ALTHOUGH HE REACHED 6,000 FEET IN THE AIR BEFORE LOSING CONTACT WITH THE UAND LATER HE WAS SADLY FOUND DEAD AT SEA. *CALCULATED RISKS, PEOPLE!*

IN WWII, THE PRISONERS KEPT IN CANADA WERE ALLOWED TO PLAY FOOTBALL AND ALL HAD A GREAT SOCIAL LIFE. SO MUCH SO, THAT WHEN THE WAR WAS OVER, A LARGE AMOUNT OF SOLDIERS DIDN'T WANT TO LEAVE. *THEY MUST HAVE BEEN LIVING THE DREAM ALRIGHT.*

AROUND 300 BC, THE MAYAN PEOPLE THOUGHT TURKEYS WERE A VESSEL OF GOD. THEY SAW TURKEYS AS A SYMBOL OF POWER AND PRESTIGE. *AH, SO THAT'S WHY I FEEL SO GOOD AFTER A THANKSGIVING DINNER...*

ANIMAL HANDLERS IN 2007 FROM THE OREGON ZOO TOOK A NEWLY ADOPTED ELEPHANT CALLED CHENDRA AROUND THE ZOO. CHENDRA STOPPED DURING HER TOUR AND BECAME FRIENDS WITH ONE OF THE SEA LIONS.

THERE IS A KNIFE AND FORK HYBRID CALLED A NORK.

IN 2011, ANGELA DUCKWORTH CONDUCTED A STUDY WHICH PROVED THAT IQ TESTS CAN BE AFFECTED BY MOTIVATION. THEY DECIDED TO PROMISE PARTICIPANTS MONETARY REWARDS DEPENDING ON WHAT THEY SCORED. THE RESULT SHOWED THAT THERE WAS A POSITIVE CORRELATION BETWEEN THE LEVEL OF REWARD AND IQ RESULT. *AH, SO THAT'S WHY MY IQ SCORES WAS SO LOW...THERE WAS NO MONEY INVOLVED.*

THERE IS A FISH CALLED THE GOLIATH TIGERFISH WHICH IS THE LARGEST TYPE OF TIGERFISH IN THE WORLD. IT'S SO BIG THAT THEY HAVE EVEN BEEN SPOTTED ATTACKING BOTH HUMANS AND CROCODILES.

AFTER HURRICANE KATRINA, THE EMIR OF QATAR DECIDED TO HELP OUT THE NATION BY DONATING OVER 100 MILLION DOLLARS, HELPING WITH THE REBUILDING OF THE HOUSING, HOSPITAL AND SCHOOL. *MONEY WELL SPENT.*

AN AUSTRALIAN MAN CALLED JAMES HARRISON STARTED DONATING BLOOD FROM A VERY YOUNG AGE - 18. THIS IS BECAUSE SOMEONE DONATED BLOOD TO HIM WHEN HE WAS A BABY WHICH SAVED HIS LIFE. FUNNILY ENOUGH JAMES BLOOD CONTAINED VERY STRONG ANTIBODIES WHICH CAN CURE RHESUS, A DISEASE THAT DESTROYS A WOMAN'S RED BLOOD CELLS WHEN THEY ARE PREGNANT. JAMES HAS DONATED BLOOD OVER 1000 TIMES, SAVING THOUSANDS OF BABIES WITH THE DISEASE.

DOGS, AND CATS ARE A LOT SMARTER THAN YOU MIGHT THINK. NOT ONLY DO THEY RECOGNISE THEIR NAME, BUT THEY ARE ALSO SMART ENOUGH TO PRETEND TO BE SICK JUST TO GET MORE ATTENTION FROM THEIR OWNER. *SOUNDS LIKE MY GIRLFRIEND*.

THE LUNA MOTH CAN'T EAT DUE TO THE SIMPLE FACT THEY DON'T HAVE MOUTHS. LUNA MOTHS ONLY LIVE FOR ABOUT A WEEK, ITS SOLE PURPOSE BEING TO MATE.

LOBSTERS MAY HAVE THE STRANGEST ANATOMY EVER. THEIR BRAINS ARE LOCATED IN THEIR THROAT, THEIR NERVOUS SYSTEM ARE IN THEIR ABDOMENS, THEIR TEETH ARE IN THEIR STOMACH...I'LL REPEAT: THEIR BRAINS ARE IN THEIR THROATS. OH, AND THEIR KIDNEYS ARE IN THEIR HEAD. *ABSOLUTELY ALIEN.*

WHEN I SAY RUM, YOU MOST LIKELY THINK OF CAPTAIN MORGAN. WELL DID YOU KNOW THAT CAPTAIN MORGAN WAS AN ENGLISH PRIVATEER WHO FOUGHT AGAINST SPAIN IN THE CARIBBEAN DURING THE 1660S AND 70S. KING CHARLES II KNIGHTED CAPTAIN MORGAN, WHOSE REAL NAME WAS HENRY. *I DON'T KNOW WHY, BUT HENRY SOUNDS LIKE SUCH A FITTING NAME.*

YOU COULD GET FREE PARKING, FREE CHARGING AND THE USE OF BUS LANES IF YOU OWNED AN ELECTRIC CAR IN NORWAY. THIS WAS AN INCENTIVE CREATED BY THE GOVERNMENT TO ENCOURAGE MORE PEOPLE TO USE ELECTRIC CARS AND BE CARBON FRIENDLY. THIS OF COURSE, CAUSED A MASSIVE INCREASE IN THE AMOUNT OF PEOPLE USING ELECTRIC CARS IN NORWAY, SO THE INCENTIVE HAD TO BE ROLLED BACK. *NOTHING LASTS FOREVER.*

IF YOU ARE A PERSON WHO STRUGGLES TO GET TO SLEEP AND FIND THAT YOUR SLEEP RHYTHM IS WAY OFF BALANCE, YOU SHOULD TRY CAMPING ONCE A WEEK. STUDIES HAVE SHOWN THAT CAMPING SOMEWHERE THERE'S NATURAL SUNLIGHT IS ENOUGH TO RESET YOUR BODY'S NATURAL CLOCK. *THE MORE YOU KNOW. UNFORTUNATELY, I'VE NEVER BEEN A FAN OF CAMPING.*

THERE IS A FACIAL RECOGNITION FOR CATS, MADE BY AN ENTREPRENEUR NAMED MU-CHI SUNG.

THE POWER OF LOVE WAS THE FIRST EVER 3D PICTURE FILM. IT WAS FIRST RELEASED IN 1992, IN LOS ANGELES.

GLOBAL WARMING IS CAUSING POLAR BEARS' HABITATS TO MELT, FORCING THEM TO FIND SHELTER ELSEWHERE. THEY ARE HAVING TO MATE WITH GRIZZLY BEARS TO FORM A HYBRID KNOWN AS A PIZZLY BEARS.

THERE WAS A RUSSIAN HITMAN CALLED ALEXANDER SOLANKI WHO WAS NICKNAMED 'THE SUPER KILLER'. HE BUILT UP A VERY IMPRESSIVE PORTFOLIO, KILLING OVER 30 MOB BOSSES BEFORE EVENTUALLY BECOMING ONE HIMSELF.

GET THIS...IN GERMANY, THERE WAS A 5.6 KILOMETRE RACE ORGANISED BETWEEN A PIGEON KEEPER AND A BEEKEEPER. THE KEEPERS CHALLENGED EACH OTHER'S CREATURE TO SEE WHO WOULD WIN IN A RACE. BEE VS BIRD. GUESS WHO WON... THE BEE BY 25 SECONDS. *I MEAN, TALK ABOUT A PISSING CONTEST...*

BEAVERS SOMETIMES HAVE ANAL SECRETION, WHICH IS CALLED CASTOREUM. THEY USE THIS TO MARK THEIR TERRITORY. ALTHOUGH IT DOESN'T SOUND NICE, THIS ANAL SECRETION SUPPOSEDLY SMELLS LIKE VANILLA AND IS OFTEN USED IN FOODS AND PERFUMES. THIS IS WHAT THEY CALLED NATURAL FLAVOURS. *YOU WON'T FIND ME MUNCHING ON ANY NATURAL FLAVOURS.*

FOOD FOR THE POOR IS A CHARITY ORGANISATION WHO GIVE AWAY FOOD TO… YOU GUESSED IT, THE POOR. OVER 95% OF THEIR PROCEEDS ARE DONATED. FUNNILY ENOUGH, THE CEO OF THE ORGANISATION IS CALLED ROBIN MAHFOOD. *IS THAT SKETCHY OR NAH?*

THE 1960S WAS THE PEAK OF TOBACCO USE, WITH OVER 40% OF THE AMERICAN POPULATION BEING REGULAR SMOKERS. DURING THIS TIME, THERE WERE MANY ADVERTS OF DOCTORS, DENTIST AND PEOPLE FROM ALL OVER DIFFERENT RESPECTED LINES WORK GLAMOURISING SMOKING. *GOD WE WERE SO WRONG.*

IN HOLLAND, IT MIGHT AS WELL BE A BIRTHDAY TO THE ENTIRE FAMILY AS IT'S TRADITION TO CONGRATULATE THE FAMILY AS WELL AS THE PERSON WHOSE BIRTHDAY IT IS. *THAT'S ACTUALLY QUITE A NICE CUSTOM.*

JOE MURPHY

LORD BRYON, A FAMOUS POET, WAS
AWFULLY UPSET AT THE FACT THAT HIS
COLLEGE WEREN'T ALLOWING DOGS ON
THE CAMPUS, SO HE CHOSE THE NEXT BEST
OPTION. HE KEPT A BEAR IN HIS COLLEGE
DORMITORY.

IN APRIL 2004, THE DANISH GOVERNMENT
RE-CREATED THEIR ENTIRE COUNTRY IN
THE GAME MINECRAFT. HAVE A GUESS HOW
MANY BUILDING BLOCKS THEY HAD TO USE
TO RE-CREATE THE ENTIRE COUNTRY....4
TRILLION MINECRAFT BUILDING BLOCKS.
AMERICAN GAMERS WOULD LATER COME
TO INVADE THE ONLINE STRUCTURE,
PUTTING AMERICAN FLAGS EVERYWHERE.
IMAGINE FINDING OUT THIS IS WHAT YOUR
GOVERNMENT HAVE BEEN UP TO.

THE PC GAME HALO 2 HAD TO BE DELAYED DUE TO THE FACT ONE OF THE KEY DEVELOPERS WHO WORKED ON THE PROJECT DECIDED TO HIDE A PICTURE OF HIS ARSE CHEEKS IN THE GAME. THIS WAS ONLY FOUND IN POST-PRODUCTION. *CAN'T LIE, THAT'S JOKES.*

INSTEAD OF ASKING TO GOOGLE WHAT THE WEATHER WILL BE LIKE TODAY, WHY NOT TAKE YOUR CUP OF COFFEE OUTSIDE AND HAVE A LOOK AT THE BUBBLES. HIGH ATMOSPHERIC PRESSURE IS ABLE TO AFFECT THE ACTUAL BUBBLES IN YOUR COFFEE. IF THE BUBBLES ARE CLOSER TO THE MIDDLE, YOU CAN EXPECT STORMY WEATHER. *IT'S NOT PRACTICAL BUT IT'S COOL, RIGHT?*

IN 1862 SLAVE NAMED ROBERT SMALLS MANAGED TO FIGHT FOR HIS FREEDOM. HE DID THIS BY SEIZING A CONFEDERATE SHIP AND DELIVERING IT TO THE UNION. DOING THIS, HE WAS PROMOTED AND BECAME A MAJOR GENERAL. HE EVENTUALLY BOUGHT THE HOUSE THAT HE WAS ENSLAVED TO AND GOT TO REUNITE WITH HIS MOTHER. *FIRSTLY, F*CK SLAVERY... SECONDLY, WHO SAYS HARD WORK DOESN'T PAY OFF?*

THE AVERAGE TREE IS MADE UP OF AROUND 99% DEAD CELLS, WITH ONLY ABOUT 1% OF A TREE BEING ALIVE AT ANY GIVEN TIME. *I FEEL LIKE A TREE SOMETIMES.*

THERE WAS SECRET SEX TAPES OF THE LATE INDONESIAN PRESIDENT ACHMED SUKARNO. THE TAPES WERE RECORDED BY THE KBG WHO ARE GENERALLY DEFINED AS THE OFFICIAL SOVIET PUBLICATION. THEIR ROLE ENCOMPASSES DIFFERENT AREAS SUCH AS THE STRUGGLE AGAINST FOREIGN SPIES AND AGENTS, THE EXPOSURE AND THE INVESTIGATION OF POLITICIANS AND ECONOMIC CRIMES BY CITIZENS, AND LOTS MORE. ANYWAY, THE KGB USED THESE RECORDINGS TO TRY AND BLACKMAIL THE PRESIDENT. HOWEVER, THIS SWIFTLY BACKFIRED AS THE PRESIDENT WASN'T ASHAMED AT ALL BUT RATHER IMPRESSED AND WOULD ON TO REQUEST COPIES FOR HIMSELF. *WHAT A STUD.*

IN THE UNITED STATES IN 2013, THE *KIDS WISH NETWORK* WAS CALLED THE WORST CHARITY IN AMERICA. THIS IS DUE TO THE FACT ONLY 3 CENTS PER DOLLAR DONATED ACTUALLY WENT TO THE CHILDREN IN NEED. *A BACKWARDS ROBIN HOOD.*

THE FAST FOOD RESTAURANT *SHAWARMA'S* WOULD SEE THEIR SALES SKYROCKET AFTER THE AVENGERS MOVIE CAME OUT. ONE OF THE LAST SCENES IN THE MOVIE WAS THE ENTIRE ORIGINAL AVENGERS TEAM, CAPTAIN AMERICA, HULK, THOR, IRONMAN, HAWK MAN AND BLACK WIDOW EATING AT THE RESTAURANT AFTER THE BIG BATTLE IN NEW YORK...*I KNOW SORRY... I'M NERDING OUT. GREAT FILM BY THE WAY, I WOULD HIGHLY RECOMMEND.*

THE SMALLEST DOG IN THE UNITED KINGDOM IS CALLED TYSON. HE ONLY WEIGHS 13 OUNCES AND IS 10 CENTIMETRES TALL.

IN 1835, THE US PRESIDENT AT THE TIME, ANDREW JACKSON WAS ABLE TO PAY OUT AMERICA'S ENTIRE DEBT. THIS WAS THE ONLY TIME IN AMERICA'S HISTORY WHERE THE COUNTRY WAS ENTIRELY DEBT FREE. THIS LASTED A YEAR. TODAY, AMERICA HAS ACCUMULATED A DEBT OF 27 TRILLION. *I WILL NEVER UNDERSTAND ECONOMICS.*

SILK PRODUCTION WAS SEEN AS ONE OF THE MOST VALUABLE THINGS IN TERMS OF FABRIC PRODUCTION. SO MUCH SO, THAT THE CHINESE KEPT IT A SECRET FOR OVER 3,000 YEARS. IF YOU WERE TO BREAK THE SECRET DURING THAT TIME, YOU COULD LEGALLY BE SENTENCED TO DEATH. OF COURSE, THE PRODUCTION OF SILK IS NOW KNOWN AS SERICULTURE, AND OCCURS THROUGH THE CULTIVATION OF SILKWORMS ON MULBERRY LEAVES. *GROSS.*

A MAN IN SAUDI ARABIA INSTALLED A COMMUNITY FRIDGE JUST OUTSIDE HIS HOME. HE WOULD ASK PEOPLE WHO LIVED AROUND HIS NEIGHBOURHOOD TO DONATE FOOD, SO THAT THE POOR COMMUNITY WOULDN'T HAVE TO BEG. *A MAN WITH A KIND HEART; WHY CAN'T WE HAVE MORE PEOPLE LIKE THAT IN THE WORLD?*

WE ALL HAVE A MATE WHO IMMEDIATELY DISAPPEARS ONCE THEY GET A GIRLFRIEND. WELL, A STUDY CONDUCTED BY HARVARD UNIVERSITY SHOWS THAT FOR EACH NEW LOVER YOU HAVE IN YOUR LIFE, YOU LOSE TWO CLOSE FRIENDS.

BUDAPEST BROKE THE WORLD RECORD FOR THE LONGEST LEGO TOWER EVER BUILT IN 2014. THE LEGO BUILDING STOOD AT 34.7 METERS TALL AND WAS MADE UP OF 150,000 COLOURFUL CUBES. *STARTING TO GET A BETTER IDEA OF WHAT GOVERNMENTS DO FOR FUN...*

TO PROTECT THE THE WATER IN LA, OVER 90 MILLION HOLLOW BLACK BALLS WERE DISTRIBUTED. THIS ARRANGEMENT WAS MADE TO TRY AND PREVENT DIRECT SUNLIGHT FROM HITTING THE WATER, IN HOPES THAT THE BALLS WILL SHADE AND COOL THE WATER, SLOWING EVAPORATION FROM THE RESERVOIR. THIS WOULD DECREASE THE DEVELOPMENT OF ALGAE, BACTERIA AND OTHER POTENTIALLY DANGEROUS CHEMICAL REACTIONS.

SIMONA HALEP IS A ROMANIAN TENNIS PLAYER WHO WAS 34 DD IN BRA SIZE. SHE DECIDED TO GO TO THE SURGEONS TO GET BREAST REDUCTION, AS HER BREAST WERE TOO BIG AND WERE IMPAIRING HER ABILITY TO PERFORM. TO SAY THE LEAST, IT WAS THE RIGHT CHOICE; SINCE HER REDUCTION, SHE HAS CLIMBED HER WAY UP THE RANKS IN WOMEN'S TENNIS. *DEDICATION.*

ON DECEMBER THE 17TH 1967, AUSTRALIA LOST THEIR PRIME MINISTER, HAROLD HOLT. HE SUPPOSEDLY WENT FOR A SWIM AND NEVER CAME BACK. *IT MUST HAVE BEEN THE REPTILES.*

ONSEN KEIUNKAN IN JAPAN IS THE OLDEST HOTEL IN THE WORLD. IT WAS FOUNDED IN 105 AD. THE EXACT SAME TWO FAMILIES HAVE OPERATED THE HOTEL SINCE.

THERE HAVE BEEN MANY THINGS BOTH PAST AND PRESENT WHICH HAVE SYMBOLISED POWER AND WEALTH.. IN THE 1800S, IT WAS PINEAPPLES. PINEAPPLES WERE A SIGN OF PRESTIGE. THIS WAS GENERALLY ACCEPTED IN ENGLAND. PEOPLE WOULD EVEN GO OUT OF THEIR WAY TO RENT PINEAPPLES FOR PARTIES.

HONEYPOT ANTS SUBMERGE THEMSELVES
IN FOOD. THIS IS A TACTIC THEY USE TO
HELP OTHER ANTS IN THEIR CLAN EXTRACT
NUTRIENTS FROM THE SURFACE OF THEIR
BODIES AND IS A PROCESS KNOWN AS
TROPHALLAXIS. *SHARING IS CARING!*

IF YOU WANT TO GET A TEST TO FIND OUT
IF YOU'RE DYSLEXIC YOU HAVE TO PAY
ROUGHLY $600 TO BE DIAGNOSED.

STUDIES HAVE SHOWN THAT SOME PEOPLE
WHO COMPLAIN A LOT CAN ACTUALLY LIVE
TWO YEARS LONGER THAN THE AVERAGE
PERSON. STUDIES SUGGEST THIS IS DUE TO
THEM CONSTANTLY LETTING OFF ANY BUILT
UP TENSION, WHICH IN TURN INCREASES
IMMUNITY AND BOOSTS OVERALL HEALTH.

DUBAI'S 'MALL OF THE WORLD' WILL BE THE WORLD'S FIRST CLIMATE-CONTROLLED INDOOR CITY. UNVEILED PLANS FOR THE MALL OF THE WORLD DEPICT A 48 MILLION SQUARE FOOT INDOOR CITY. *THAT IS SOME NEXT LEVEL SHIT.*

THE AVOCADO IS THE WORLD'S MOST NUTRITIOUS FRUIT WITH OVER 25 ESSENTIAL NUTRIENTS.

IN CHONGQING IN CHINA, THERE IS A VERY POPULAR TOURIST LOCATION WHERE THE SIDEWALKS HAVE TWO SEPARATE LANES; ONE FOR PEOPLE WHO WALK AND GO ON THEIR PHONE, ONE FOR THOSE WHO DON'T. *SO, THIS IS WHAT THE WORLD HAS COME TO...*

IN THE UNITED STATES THERE WAS A NATIONWIDE BAN ON PRODUCTION, IMPORTATION, TRANSPORTATION, AND SALES OF ALCOHOLIC BEVERAGES FROM 1920-1933. LAW OFFICIALS GOT DESPERATE WHEN PEOPLE WERE IGNORING THE LAWS. SO, THEY BEGAN POISONING THE DRINKS AS A DETERRENT. *GOD DAMN IT, THE US GOVERNMENT HAVE DONE SOME SKETCHY STUFF.*

CELLULAR MEMORY IS A PHENOMENON WHICH HAPPENS WHEN YOU GET AN ORGAN TRANSPLANT. YOU BEGIN TO EXPERIENCE SIMILAR THOUGHTS AND START TO HAVE SIMILAR CRAVINGS TO THE ONES YOUR DONOR HAD. IT HAS ALSO BEEN DOCUMENTED THAT A SMALL PORTION OF PEOPLE WHO HAVE HAD ORGAN TRANSPLANT EXPERIENCE A CHANGED PERSONALITY. *I'M TELLING YOU, WE ARE ALL LINKED IN SOME FUNKY WAY.*

THE MULTINATIONAL PHARMACEUTICAL COMPANY *BAYER* INTRODUCED A DRUG IN 1898 KNOWN AS DIACETYLMORPHINE. IT WAS MARKETED TO TREAT PEOPLE WITH MORPHINE ADDICTION. DIACETYLMORPHINE IS BETTER KNOWN TODAY AS THE STREET DRUG...HAVE A GUESS. HEROIN. *OH AMERICA, YOU NEVER FAIL TO AMAZE ME.*

SCIENTIST HAVE NOW PROVEN THAT COLD SHOWERS ARE A HEALTHIER OPTION THAN WARM. IT DRASTICALLY IMPROVES YOUR IMMUNITY, BLOOD CIRCULATION, RELIEVES DEPRESSION AND HAS BEEN SHOWN TO EASE ACNE. *NOT THAT YOU CARE, BUT I'VE ALSO RECENTLY STARTED COLD SHOWERS... IT'S GONNA TAKE SOME GETTING USED TO...*

IN THE 1990S, THERE WAS A MASSIVE POWER OUTAGE IN NEW YORK. THE PEOPLE OF NEW YORK WOULD LOOK UP TO SEE STRANGE CLOUDS SHINING AT NIGHT IN SKY, UNAWARE THEY WERE STARING AT THE MILKY WAY. HOWEVER, DUE TO THE FACT WE NOW HAVE SO MUCH LIGHT POLLUTION, IT'S UNLIKELY WE'LL GET ANOTHER CHANCE TO SEE MILKY WAY GALAXY. *THAT BREAKS MY HEART. JUST IMAGINE HOW COOL THAT WOULD HAVE BEEN!*

THERE WAS AN ARTIFICIAL INTELLIGENT COMPUTER CALLED WATSON IN IBM WHO LEARNED HOW TO SWEAR USING THE URBAN DICTIONARY. WHEN SPOKEN TO, WATSON WOULD OCCASIONALLY USE SLANG AND CURSE, SO THE SCIENTIST HAD TO REMOVE THE ENTIRE URBAN DICTIONARY FROM THE COMPUTER'S DATABASE. *WHAT'S A COMPUTER GOTTA DO TO HAVE SOME FUN ROUND HERE?*

YOU MAY HAVE HEARD THIS ONE BEFORE, BUT THE IRONY OF IT WILL REMAIN TIMELESS. THE PEOPLE WHO BUILT THE *TITANIC* FAMOUSLY CALLED IT THE 'UNSINKABLE SHIP'. *WELL, I THINK WE ALL KNOW HOW THAT WENT.*

THE BRITISH AMY MANAGED TO PERFECT THE ART OF BREWING TEA IN AN ARMED VESSEL KNOWN AS THE 'BRITISH ARMY BOILING VESSEL'.

THE CURRENT PRESIDENT OF THE PHILIPPINES, RODRIGO DUTERTE, MANAGED TO MAKE THE CITY ONE OF THE HAPPIEST PLACES IN THE WHOLE OF SOUTH EAST ASIA. HE WAS DUBBED THE PUNISHER BY *TIMES MAGAZINE* DUE TO THE FACT HE WENT AFTER ALL THE DRUG LORDS AND KILLED THEM. *SOUNDS LIKE THE PUNISHER ALRIGHT...*

BAGHDAD IS THE LOCATION POINT FOR THE BIGGEST AND THE MOST EXPENSIVE EMBASSY IN THE WORLD, OWNED BY THE US. THE EMBASSY SPANS A WHOPPING 104 ACRES AND COST.... 750 MILLION DOLLARS TO BUILD.

IN A RECENT STUDY, THE BOTTLENOSE DOLPHINS WERE SHOWN TO HAVE ONE OF THE LONGEST MEMORIES IN THE ENTIRE ANIMAL KINGDOM. THEY CAN RECOGNISE OTHER DOLPHIN'S WHISTLES EVEN AFTER 20 YEARS OF BEING APART.

ALTHOUGH WOLVERINES ARE RELATIVELY SMALL, THEY HAVE BEEN SHOWN TO BE ABLE TO ATTACK ELK AND OTHER LARGER ANIMALS. *MUST BE EASY WHEN YOU HAVE REGENERATIVE POWER...*

RECENT DATA THAT WAS COLLECTED HAS SHOWN THAT 100 ACRES OF PIZZA IS SERVED EACH DAY IN AMERICA. *ARE YOU A FAN OF PIZZA? YEAH OF COURSE YOU ARE.*

YOU CAN FIND DNA TRACES FROM
CIGARETTES BUTTS.

STUDIES HAVE SHOWN THAT A 45 TO 50
MINUTE NAP DURING THE DAY INCREASES
COGNITIVE FUNCTION WHICH HAS
POSITIVE EFFECT ON YOUR MEMORY AND
LEARNING ABILITY. *I MIGHT HAVE TO START
USING THIS EXCUSE AT UNIVERSITY.*

YOU KNOW THAT GUY STEPHEN HAWKING?
NO, I'M NOT GOING TO TALK ABOUT SPACE.
STEVEN IS THE ONLY PERSON TO DATE
WHO HAS PLAYED THEMSELVES IN *STAR
TREK. R.I.P STEPHEN HAWKING.*

THERE IS A 16-STORY OFFICE BUILDING
CALLED THE GATE TOWER BUILDING. THE
GATE TOWER BUILDING HAS AN ENTIRE
HIGHWAY PASSING THROUGH THE 5TH, 6TH
AND 7TH FLOOR OF THE STRUCTURE. THIS
BUILDING IS IN OSAKA, JAPAN.

THERE WAS A CHRISTMAS TRUCE DURING WWI IN 1914; THE GERMAN AND BRITISH TROOPS MET OVER NO MAN'S LAND AND WERE ABLE TO SOCIALISE FREELY WITHOUT FEAR OF BEING SHOT DEAD - THEY SANG CAROLS, SHARED CIGARETTES AND EVEN PLAYED FOOTBALL. TODAY, THAT MOMENT IS STILL SEEN AS ONE OF THE MOST PEACEFUL ACTS CONDUCTED AROUND THE MOST VIOLENT TIMES. *CHRISTMAS REALLY IS A TIME OF MIRACLES.*

THE DEA REPORTED SEIZING 477 MILLION DOLLARS WORTH OF DRUGS IN 2005. HOWEVER, THE TOTAL VALUE OF THE DRUG TRADE IN 2005 WAS 320 BILLION. *TALK ABOUT DOING A SH*T JOB.*

AROUND 150 BILLION WAS SPENT ON CANNABIS, COCAINE, HEROIN AND METHAMPHETAMINE BY AMERICANS IN 2016. *THAT'S A LOT OF DRUGS.*

A KOREAN MAN CALLED CHOI GA FUNG ESCAPED PRISON JUST AFTER 5 DAYS. HE WAS ABLE TO FIT THROUGH A SLOT WHILST THE GUARDS WERE SLEEPING. HE HAD 5 YEARS OF YOGA EXPERIENCE.

HAVE YOU EVER NOTICED THE WHITE SPOT ON YOUR FINGERNAIL AND WONDERED WHAT IT MIGHT BE? THOSE WHITE SPOTS ARE COMMONLY CONFUSED AND ARE SEEN AS A SIGN UP SOME FORM OF DEFICIENCY BUT THEY ARE ACTUALLY CAUSED MINOR BRUISING THAT HAPPENS WHEN YOUR NAILS ARE GROWING AND ARE PERFECTLY NORMAL. IT'S CALLED LEUKONYCHIA.

IN AMERICA THERE IS A ROAD CALLED ROUTE FOOT AND IT HAS BEEN NICKED NAMED THE LONGEST ROAD IN AMERICA DUE TO HOW LONG IT IS.

TWO PLANES DIRECTLY COLLIDED IN SEPTEMBER OF 1940, OVER BROCKLESBY AUSTRALIA. LUCKILY, THESE TWO PLANES BECAME INTERLOCKED. THE ENGINE OF THE TOP PLANE STOPPED WORKING WHILST THE BOTTOM'S STAYED INTACT. THIS MEANT THAT THE PILOT WHO WAS IN CONTROL OF THE BOTTOM PLANE WAS ABLE TO SAFELY LAND THE PLANES AND ALL THE CREW MEN ON BOARD SURVIVED.

DID YOU KNOW THAT POTATOES ARE ABLE TO ABSORB THE SUBSEQUENTLY REFLECT MICROWAVE SIGNALS THE SAME WAY THAT HUMAN BODIES DO? *TALK ABOUT MULTITASKING.*

THERE ARE NOW MANY SCIENTISTS SUGGESTING THAT WE HAVE WAY MORE THAN FIVE BASIC SENSES. THESE INCLUDE THINGS LIKE MAGNETORECEPTION WHICH IS THE ABILITY TO DETECT MAGNETIC FIELDS. AND ONE THAT WE MIGHT ALL TOO FAMILIAR WITH, CHRONOCEPTION WHICH THE SENSE OF TIME PASSING.

A BANK WORKER ONCE TRANSFERRED 222,222,222 EUROS AFTER FALLING ASLEEP ON HER DESK. SHE SENT THE MONEY TO AN ACCOUNT THAT WAS ONLY MEANT TO RECEIVE 60 EUROS. FUNNILY ENOUGH, SHE WASN'T FIRED, BUT HER CO-PARTNER WAS DUE TO THE FACT HE DIDN'T SPOT THE MISTAKE. *IT'S CHRISTMAS EVERYDAY FOR SOMEONE'S BANK ACCOUNT.*

ACCORDING TO SOME EXPERTS, IT CAN COST ANYWHERE FROM 14-30 DOLLARS TO MAKE A PAIR OF BEATS BY DOCTOR DRE. THIS IS AN INSANE PROFIT MARGIN WHEN YOU THINK THAT THE AVERAGE COST OF A PAIR OF BEATS BY DRE IS ROUGHLY $200.

RICHARD SHASE WAS A SERIAL KILLER IN THE LATE 1970S. RICHARD EXPLAINED THAT HE WOULD ONLY BREAK INTO HOUSES WHICH WERE OPEN. HE SAID: "IF THE DOORS ARE OPEN, THEN I AM WELCOMED. IF THEY ARE CLOSED, THEN I AM NOT" *F*CK THAT GUY.*

DID YOU KNOW THAT WE DON'T THINK OF FOOD AS TOO SWEET UNTIL OUR BONES STOP GROWING? HENCE WHY KIDS HAVE A CRAZY SWEET TOOTH.

SHAKESPEARE'S FATHER HELD A LOT OF DIFFERENT JOBS, AND AT ONE POINT GOT PAID TO DRINK BEER. *WHERE DO I SIGN UP?*

JACK THE RIPPER WAS AN ENGLISH SERIAL KILLER. BETWEEN AUGUST AND NOVEMBER 1888, HE MURDERED AT LEAST FIVE WOMEN - ALL PROSTITUTES - IN OR NEAR THE WHITECHAPEL DISTRICT OF LONDON'S EAST END. JACK THE RIPPER WAS NEVER IDENTIFIED OR ARRESTED. *SOUNDS LIKE SOMEONE NEEDED TO GET LAID.*

MOST PILOTS ON AIRLINES ARE ADVISED TO EAT COMPLETELY DIFFERENT MEALS FOR THE 'OFF CHANCE' THAT THE FOOD HAS FOOD POISONING.

SOME OF THE MOST EXOTIC ANIMALS AND
ORGANISMS ON THE PLANET ARE FOUND IN
MADAGASCAR. ROUGHLY 90% OF ALL THE
PLANTS AND ANIMALS WHICH INHABIT THE
AREA ARE KNOWN AS ENDEMIC SPECIES.
THIS MEANS THEY ARE UNIQUELY TIED TO
THE GEOGRAPHICAL LOCATION AND CAN'T
BE FOUND ELSEWHERE IN THE WORLD.
THAT'S PRETTY GODDAMN AWESOME.

IN 2005, THE GOLDEN STATE FENCE
COMPANY IN SOUTHERN CALIFORNIA
WHERE FINED 5 MILLION FOR EMPLOYING
ILLEGAL IMMIGRANTS TO WORK AND HELP
BUILD THE FENCES.

WHEN YOU EARN YOUR PHD IN FINLAND
YOU ARE GIVEN A DOCTORAL HAT, AS WELL
AS A SWORD.

I'M SURE YOU'VE HEARD OF COCA COLA, BUT DID YOU KNOW THAT THEY HAVE ACTUALLY MADE OVER... HAVE A GUESS...IS IT 500, 1000, OR OVER 3000 DIFFERENT TYPES OF BEVERAGES? THAT'S RIGHT, COCA COLA HAVE MADE OVER 3000 DIFFERENT TYPES OF BEVERAGES.

DID YOU KNOW PURPLE EYES EXIST? THEY'RE CAUSED BY A DISORDER KNOWN AS ALEXANDRIA'S GENESIS WHICH ALSO COMES WITH MUCH PALER SKIN. BONUS FACT, DID YOU ALSO KNOW THAT IT IS POSSIBLE FOR INDIVIDUALS TO HAVE TWO DIFFERENT EYE COLOURS - IT;S A CONDITION KNOWN AS HETEROCHROMIA IRIDIUM.

MARINE ALGAE ARE SEEN AS THE MOST IMPORTANT ORGANISM IN WORLD. THIS IS DUE TO THAT FACT MARINE ALGAE PRODUCES ROUGHLY 70-80% OF THE OXYGEN WE BREATH IN. *THINK WE CAN ALL AGREE THAT SOUNDS ABOUT RIGHT...O2 IS PRETTY IMPORTANT RIGHT?*

IN CAPETOWN, SOUTH AFRICA DURING THE 1800S, A RAILWAY WORKER NAMED JAMES EDWIN WIDE SAW A BABOON DRIVING AN OXCART AT A MARKET AND DECIDED TO EMPLOY HIM AT THE RAILWAY TO OPERATE RAILWAY SIGNALS. HE MADE HIM HIS PERSONAL ASSISTANT AND NAMED HIM JACK. JACK WAS SURPRISINGLY GOOD AT HIS JOB AND WORKED FOR THE RAILROAD UNTIL HE DIED. *TALK ABOUT ANIMAL CRUELTY, POOR BABOON DIDN'T EVEN GET A PENSION OR RETIREMENT PLAN.*

OVER 2000 WORDS WERE ADDED TO THE ENGLISH DICTIONARY BY JUST ONE MAN, HAVE A GUESS WHO? GO ON, I'LL GIVE YOU 5 SECONDS TO HAVE A THINK… OF COURSE, IT WAS THE ONE AND ONLY WILLIAM SHAKESPEARE. SHAKESPEARE INTRODUCED WORDS LIKE NEW-FANGLED, SWAGGER AND BEDAZZLED. *SWAGGER…*

OVER 2,000 TONS OF UNEXPLODED BOMBS ARE FOUND EVERY YEAR IN GERMANY. BEFORE A NEW CONSTRUCTION IS BUILT IN GERMANY THE SITE MUST UNDERGO A SEVERE CHECK. *FUCK THAT SH*T.*

IF YOU COMMIT ANY FORM OF CRIME IN THE SEAS, THEN YOU ARE CONSIDERED A PIRATE.

SINCE 1971, BHUTAN HAS BEEN MEASURING ITS YEARLY DEVELOPMENT AND PROSPERITY BY ITS GROSS NATIONAL HAPPINESS SCORED, RATHER THAN USING GROSS NATURAL PRODUCT PRODUCED. IT'S THE ONLY COUNTRY THAT DOES SO.

THOUGH LOOKS, ENERGY, AND MENTAL EFFICIENCY MAY DECLINE, STUDIES HAVE INDICATED THAT PEOPLE GENERALLY BECOME HAPPIER AS THEY GET OLDER. LEVELS OF HAPPINESS AND EMOTIONAL WELLBEING TEND TO RISE.

IT'S BEEN SHOWN THAT BLOOD CONTAINS SIMILAR COMPONENTS TO EGGS AND CAN BE USED FOR COOKING. THIS MEAN THEY CAN BE USED A SUBSTITUTE FOR MAKING ICE CREAM AND BAKING. *ONLY VAMPIRES WOULD DARE.*

APPROXIMATELY 1 BILLION VALENTINE'S DAY CARDS ARE GIVEN EACH YEAR.

IN 2005, JACKIE CHAN EXPLAINED THAT HE WAS BLACKLISTED BY INSURANCE COMPANIES DUE TO THE NATURE OF HIS STUNTS. THIS MEANS THAT IF ANYONE GETS INJURED ON SET, THE MONEY WOULD HAVE TO COME DIRECTLY FROM JACKIE CHAN'S POCKET. HE WOULD HAVE TO COVER THEIR ENTIRE MEDICAL FEES. *WHAT A GUY.*

THE US 50 AND 100 DOLLAR BILLS ARE COMMONLY COUNTERFEITED BY THE NORTH KOREAN GOVERNMENT. THESE COUNTERFEIT BILLS ARE KNOWN AS SUPERFITS. THEY ARE SO PRECISE, IT'S NEARLY INDISTINGUISHABLE WITH THE NAKED EYE.

WHEN *THE TERMINATOR* WAS BEING WRITTEN BY JAMES CAMERON, HE WAS HOMELESS. HE ENDED UP SELLING THE RIGHTS TO THE MOVIE FOR A DOLLAR. THE ONE PROPOSAL HE HAD WAS THAT HE COULD DIRECT THE MOVIE. *WELL, THAT INVESTMENT DEFINITELY CAME BACK.*

THE CREATOR OF THE FIRST EVER AMERICAN DICTIONARY WAS CALLED NOAH WEBSTER. HE LEARNED OVER 26 LANGUAGES IN ORDER TO DO DEEP RESEARCH ABOUT AMERICAN LANGUAGE FOR A BETTER UNDERSTANDING. *I BET HE WAS NEVER LOST FOR WORDS.*

DENICE FOXES MATE FOR LIFE.

INTELLIGENT DISOBEDIENCE IS A TERM
USED WHEN A GUIDE DOG GOES AGAINST
THE OWNER'S ORDER. GUARD DOGS WILL
DO THIS REGULARLY IF THEY DEEM THE
INSTRUCTION UNSAFE. *THANK GOD FOR
DOGS.*

25% OF THE WORLD'S HAZELNUT CROPS ARE
MADE AND USED SPECIFICALLY FOR
NUTELLA.

THE DEAD SEA HAS AN UNBELIEVABLY
HIGH SALT CONCENTRATION. IT HAS ABOUT
8 TO 9 TIMES MORE SALT THAN NATURAL
SEA WATER. THIS MEANS THE DEAD HAS
VERY HIGH BUOYANCY, MAKING IT VERY
EASY TO FLOAT.

IN THE 13TH CENTURY, POPE GREGORY V FAMOUSLY DECLARED A WAR ON CATS. ACCORDING TO POPE GREGORY, BLACK CATS WERE AN INSTRUMENT OF SATAN. WITH THE DECLARATION OF THE WAR ON CATS BEING CONFIRMED, THE EXTERMINATION OF CATS WOULD BE CARRIED OUT THROUGHOUT EUROPE. *MAYBE A LITTLE OVER THE TOP. AND SO MUCH FOR BEING A SHEPHERD TO OTHER ANIMALS.*

THE INDONESIAN MINISTRY OF AFFAIRS AND FISHERIES WORKED OUT THAT A SINGLE MANTA RAY, IF CAUGHT AND KILLED, IS ONLY WORTH 40-400 DOLLARS. BUT IF KEPT ALIVE, THESE BAD BOYS ARE WORTH ABOUT ONE MILLION IN TOURISM REVENUE.

DURING THE VICTORIAN TIMES IN ENGLAND, PEOPLE WOULD TAKE PICTURES OF THEIR DEAD RELATIVES IN LIFELIKE POSITIONS.

THE BUGATTI VEYRON IS THE MOST LUXURIOUS AND EXPENSIVE ON ROAD CAR TO DATE. THE AVERAGE PRICE FOR ONE OF THESE BEAUTIES IS ANYWHERE FROM 1.7 TO 3 MILLION DOLLARS. JUST THE TIRES ONLY ARE 42,000 PER SET. THE CARS CAN STAY AT TOP SPEED (254 MPH) FOR 15 MINUTES.

MOST OF THE TIME, ICE CREAM DISPLAYED ON TV COMMERCIALS IS JUST MASHED POTATO. MOST SETS ARE WAY TOO HOT AND THE ICE CREAM WOULD INEVITABLY MELT. *DON'T BELIEVE EVERYTHING YOU SEE ON TV KIDS.*

BACK IN ANCIENT GREECE, IT WAS MEN THAT WOULD MAINLY WEAR SKIRTS.

12,000 DOLLARS. THAT'S THE PRICE PAID FOR THE MOST EXPENSIVE PIZZA IN THE WORLD. THE PIZZA WAS MADE BY CHEF RENATO VIOLA WHO PREPARED THE ENTIRE DISH AT THE HOUSE. THE FISH CONTAINS CAVIAR, MEDITERRANEAN LOBSTER AND RED PRAWN. *FISH ON PIZZA….PIZZA WORTH 12,000…GODDAMN IT RENATO!*

IN FINLAND, EXPECTED MOTHERS ARE GIVEN A BOX FILLED WITH SHEETS, TOYS AND EVEN MATTRESSES. THIS IS WHERE FINLAND BABIES SLEEP. THIS IS TRADITION THAT'S BEEN GOING ON SINCE THE 1930S. *I BET BABIES ARE CONSTANTLY CRYING.*

I DON'T KNOW ABOUT YOU BUT I HAVE NEVER REALLY THOUGHT HOSPITALS ARE WELCOMING IN ANY SENSE. NEITHER DID RUSSIAN BILLIONIARE VASTLY KYLUKIN, HE DECIDED TO DESIGN A HOSPITAL WHICH LOOKS LIKE A YACHT CALLED WHITE SAILS HOSPITAL. HE WANTED TO CREATE A HOSPITAL WHICH WAS INVITING.

AS PART OF GREENLAND'S PRISON SYSTEM, THEY ALLOW FOR LARGE LIBERTIES AS A REHABILITATION SCHEME TO GET INMATES MORE PROACTIVE. THEY EVEN OFFER FREE SCHOOL AND SOME OF THESE INMATES HAVE ACCESS TO THE KEYS TO THEIR OWN CELL. *THIS IS PRISON?*

IN 2004, COMPETITIVE EATER MOLLY SCHULER MANAGED TO WIN FOUR EATING CONTESTS IN JUST 3 DAYS. AT THE TIME SHE ONLY WEIGHED ABOUT 126LBS. SHE WAS ABLE TO EAT 363 CHICKEN WINGS, 59 PANCAKES, 5 POUNDS OF BACON AND 5 POUNDS OF BARBECUE MEAT. F*CK ME THAT'S A LOT OF FOOD! *I WOULD SAY FATTY BUM BUM BUT I'M TWICE AS HEAVY.*

THERE WAS AN APP CREATED TO SOLVE ANY MATH EQUATION. THE APP IS CALLED PHOTOMATH. *IF YOU'RE IN SCHOOL…WELL THERE YOU GO.*

OVER 350 MILLION PHOTOS ARE UPLOADED TO FACEBOOK BY USERS EVERYDAY. TILL PRESENT DATE, THE TOTAL OF PHOTOS WHICH HAVE BEEN UPLOADED SINCE THE START OF FACEBOOK IN 2004 IS MORE THAN 250 BILLION.

THERE IS A WAS A MAN WAS CALLED HAMAD WHO WAS FROM ABUDBI AND HAD HIS NAMED CRAVED INTO A DESERT. THE LETTERS HE USED WERE OVER 1000 METERS LONG. *I GUESS MONEY CAN'T BUY HAPPINESS, BUT IT CAN CURE BOREDOM.*

RIGHT TO LIGHT IS A FORM OF EASEMENT IN THE ENGLISH LAW THAT GIVES A LONG-STANDING OWNER OF A BUILDING WITH WINDOWS THE RIGHT TO MAINTAIN THE LEVEL OF ILLUMINATION. THIS BASICALLY MEANS THESE BUILDING CAN REFUSE CONSTRUCTION WORK WHICH MAY PREVENT THEM FROM GETTING NATURAL LIGHT.

THE REGGAE MUSICIAN BOB MARLEY WHEN SINGING *NO WOMAN NO CRY* ACTUALLY SUNG 'NO, WOMAN, NUH CRY'. AS 'NUH' IN JAMAICAN IS SIMILAR TO 'DON'T' THIS TRANSLATES TO 'NO WOMAN, DON'T CRY'. *HE WANTED TO LET WOMEN KNOW THAT THERE'S NO NEED TO WORRY ABOUT A THING.*

A BRITISH TEENAGER CALLED RORY MCINNES THOUGHT IT WOULD BE FUNNY TO SECRETLY PAINT AN 18 METER PENIS AT THE TOP OF HIS HOUSE. THE FOLLOWING YEAR, HIS PARENTS WOULD LOOK UP THEIR HOUSE ON GOOGLE MAPS AND FIND THE GIANT PENIS PAINTING. *TOP CLASS BANTER.*

SCIENTIST SAY THAT THEY AVERAGE CUMULUS CLOUD WEIGHS AROUND 500,000 KILOGRAMS. *I THOUGHT CLOUDS WERE LIGHT AS F*CK.*

RICHARD NIXON IS THE ONLY PRESIDENT
WHO HAS EVER RESIGNED WHILST STILL IN
OFFICE. IT WAS NOTED THAT HE COULD
PLAY 5 DIFFERENT INSTRUMENTS.

DID YOU KNOW THAT IF YOU HAVE A
FRIEND MAKE YOU A SANDWICH, IT WOULD
TASTE BETTER THAN IF YOU MADE THE
SANDWICH YOURSELF WITH THE EXACT
SAME INGREDIENTS? AND NO, IT'S NOT
BECAUSE YOU'RE A BAD COOK. A
PSYCHOLOGIST EXPLAINS THAT WE
ANTICIPATE THE TASTE OF OUR OWN FOOD
BEFORE WE EAT IT, SO WHEN WE FINALLY
GET AROUND TO EATING, IT HAS A
WEAKENED EFFECT.

IN AMERICA, HALF OF ALL ONLINE
SHOPPING TAKES PLACE ON AMAZON.

THE OLYMPIC MEDAL USED TO BE THE
AWARD MEDAL FOR ART.

SOME WHITE AND ORANGE TIGERS THAT ARE LEFT IN CAPTIVITY TOGETHER END UP BREEDING WITH EACH OTHER TO MAKE GOLDEN TIGERS. THIS IS VERY RARE AS ORANGE AND WHITE TIGERS DON'T NORMALLY MATE.

A MAN CALLED WHO SUNG WIN WHO HAD KIDNEY FAILURE, CREATED HIS OWN KIDNEY DIALYSIS MACHINE TO KEEP HIM ALIVE, AS HE COULD NO LONGER PAY FOR HIS HOSPITAL FEES. HE WAS ABLE TO KEEP HIMSELF ALIVE FOR 13 YEARS.

A STORM IN A NORTH WESTERN VENEZUELA NEAR THE CATATUMBO RIVER HAS BEEN RAGING FOR CENTURIES, IT'S KNOWN AS THE EVERLASTING STORM. IT STRIKES LIGHTENING OVER 1.2 MILLION TIMES PER YEAR. *FITTING NAME.*

YOU CAN SEE YOUR FACE REFLECTION IN THE MIRROR-LIKE SALAR DE UYUNI, THE WORLD'S LARGEST SALT FLAT. IT IS 12,000 SQUARE KILOMETERS AND IS A SALT-ENCRUSTED PREHISTORIC LAKE IN POTOSI, SOUTHWEST BOLIVIA. IT'S 3,660M ABOVE SEA LEVEL.

ALL BRITISH TANKS SINCE 1945 HAVE TO BE FULLY EQUIPPED WITH A TEA-MAKING FACILITY.

VIKING NEVER ACTUALLY WORE HORNED HELMETS, THE ONLY HELMET DISCOVERED THAT BELONGED TO A VIKING DIDN'T HAVE HORNS AND WAS SIMPLY A ROUND HAT. *HATE TO BE A MYTH BUSTER.*

YASU TAKINU, A 58 YEAR OLD JAPANESE MAN, STARTED SUBDIVIDING TO TRY AND FIND HIS WIFE'S REMAINS. THE LAST WORDS OF HIS WIFE WERE "I WANT TO GO HOME" AND HE WISHES TO FULFIL THEM. *NOW THAT'S LOVE.*

WALT DISNEY WAS GIVEN A HONORARY OSCAR FOR *SNOW WHITE* IN 1938. THE STATUE HE GOT HAD AN EXTRA 7 MINI STATUES. *OF COURSE, REPRESENTING THE 7 DWARVES, SURELY THAT COUNTS FOR 7 OSCARS... NO? OKAY...*

A YOUNG MAN KNOWN AS JACKLYN LUCAS LIED HIS WAY INTO THE MILITARY AND MANAGED TO BECOME THE YOUNGEST MARINE EVER AT THE AGE OF 17. HE WON HIMSELF A MEDAL OF HONOUR AFTER JUMPING WILLINGLY ON TWO LIVE GRENADES TO PROTECT HIS SQUAD MEMBERS. *THAT'S SOME CAPTAIN AMERICA SH*T.*

IN 2014, NEW YORK CITY ANNOUNCED PLANS TO TURN ALL OF THEIR OLD PHONES BOTH INTO WIFI HOTSPOTS.

CATS HATE TO DRINK WATER NEAR THEIR FOOD SOURCE. SO, IF YOU HAVE A CAT, MAKE SURE TO KEEP THEIR WATER AND FOOD IN DIFFERENT LOCATIONS TO STOP THEM FROM GETTING TOO THIRSTY. *IMAGINE NOT BEING ABLE TO DRINK AND EAT AT THE SAME TIME.*

NINJAS NEVER ACTUALLY WORE BLACK. THE BEST COLOUR FOR NINJAS TO HAVE WEAR IN THE DARK IS NAVY.

HAVE YOU EVER NOTICED THAT OLD BOOKS HAVE A DISTINCT SMELL? THIS IS BECAUSE THEY HAVE ORGANIC COMPOUND WITHIN THE PAPER THAT BREAKS DOWN OVER TIME. THIS RELEASES SIMILAR SMELLS TO ALMONDS, GRASS AND VANILLA.

IN JAPAN, THERE ARE OVER 2000
DIFFERENT FLAVOURS OF *KITKAT*! TO NAME
A FEW: SOY SAUCE, GINGER ALE, CRÈME
BRÛLÉE, GREEN TEA AND BANANA. *NOT
SURE HOW I FEEL ABOUT A SOY SAUCE
KITKAT.*

THERE ARE ABOUT 10 QUINTILLION
INSECTS ON OUR PLANET. TO CLARIFY FOR
YOU, THAT'S 10, WITH 18 ZEROS
FOLLOWING. 10,000,000,000,000,000,000.

THE NORDIC, BY TURNING TO DIGITAL
PAYMENT ALL OVER THE COUNTRY, ARE
HOPING TO LOWER COSTS FOR
MERCHANTS, OFFER BETTER SECURITY AND
MAKE IT HARDER FOR CRIMINALS TO
LAUNDER MONEY. DUE TO THEIR
OPENNESS TO NEW TECHNOLOGY AND
TRUST IN INSTITUTIONS, THE NORDIC
COUNTRIES ARE THE PRIME CANDIDATES
TO CREATE THE WORLD'S FIRST CASHLESS
SOCIETIES. IT HAS BEEN CALCULATED THAT
THIS COULD HAPPEN BY 2023.

THERE ARE MORE TIGERS HELD IN CAPTIVITY IN THE US (5000), COMPARED THE NUMBER OF THOSE RUNNING WILD IN AFRICA - ONLY 3500 LEFT. *THIS BREAKS MY HEART.*

MICRO SLEEP IS A SYNDROME THAT OCCURS TO PEOPLE WHO ARE SLEEP DEPRIVED, ITS RELATIVELY COMMON. HOWEVER IT IS VERY DANGEROUS AND CAN QUITE EASILY OCCUR WHEN YOU'RE DRIVING.

GO ON TWITTER AND LOOK UP THE ACCOUNT BIG_BEN_CLOCK. EVERY HOUR, THE ACCOUNT TWEETS 'BONG BONG, BONG, BONG, BONG'. *MAKE OF THAT WHAT YOU WILL.*

THERE IS A CITY IN GEORGIA CALLED PEACHTREE, WHICH HAS A 145 KILOMETER NETWORK OF PATHWAYS STRICTLY DEDICATED TO GOLF CARTS.

AT GOOGLE JOB INTERVIEWS, THEY DON'T ASK TEST SCORES OR GBA SCORES. GOOGLE DOESN'T BELIEVE IT CORRELATES TO SUCCESS AT THE COMPANY.

4% OF NORMANDY BEACHES IS MADE UP OF SHRAPNEL FROM THE D-DAY LANDINGS.

AMERICA'S FIRST EVER SELF-MADE MILLIONAIRE WAS ACTUALLY A BLACK WOMAN NAME SARAR BREED LOVE. SHE MADE HER FORTUNES BY DEVELOPING A WELL RESPECTED HAIR PRODUCT WHICH HELPED PEOPLE GROW THEIR HAIR FASTER. *THINK I KNOW WHAT I'M GETTING MY BROTHER FOR CHRISTMAS THIS YEAR.*

AROUND 300,00 DOLLARS ARE SPENT EACH YEAR BY THE PENTAGON TO STUDY THE BODY LANGUAGE OF GLOBAL POLITICIANS AND LEADERS.

DID YOU KNOW THAT IN MEDIEVAL TIMES, A MOMENT WAS ACTUALLY A UNIT OF TIME AND REPRESENTED 90 SECONDS?

A CHIMP IN THE RUSSIAN ZOO IN PANDORA, BECAME A SMOKING ADDICT AND ALCOHOLIC BECAUSE SO MANY VISITORS WERE GIVING THE CHIMP 'TREATS'. THE CHIMP IN 2012 WAS TAKEN TO REHAB TO BE TREATED FOR HIS ISSUE. *YOU'LL BE GLAD TO KNOW HE'S BEEN SOBER EVER SINCE.*

IN THE 1930S, THE LETTER E WAS USED TO MARK A FAIL IN AN EXAM. HOWEVER, THIS WAS SWIFTLY CHANGED AS SOME STUDENTS MISTOOK THE E FOR EXCELLENCE. *I WOULD HAVE PAID GOOD MONEY TO SEE A STUDENT'S REACTION WHEN THEY FOUND OUT THE REAL GRADE.*

IN GERMANY, IF YOU'RE A WOMAN AND UNMARRIED BY YOUR 30TH BIRTHDAY, YOU ARE EXPECTED TO CLEAN YOUR BEST FRIENDS' DOORKNOBS, WHILST MEN WILL DO OTHER CLEANING CHORES. THE ONLY WAY OUT OF THIS WEIRD TRADITION IS TO SECURE A KISS FROM THE OPPOSITE SEX.

AMERICAN TAXPAYERS WILL SAVE ABOUT 4.4 BILLION DOLLARS OVER THE NEXT 30 YEARS BECAUSE OF THE SWITCH FROM DOLLAR BILLS TO COINS.

IN SIXTH CENTURY CHINA, THE FIRST EVER HUMAN FLIGHT WITH ARTIFICIAL WINGS WAS RECORDED. THE EMPEROR KAO YANG WOULD STRAP PRISONERS TO KITES THEN WOULD THROW THEM OFF BUILDING TO SEE IF THEY COULD FLY. *NOT A BAD WAY TO GO OUT IF YOU ASK ME.*

MIKE HAZE, A COLLEGE STUDENT, GOT A FRIEND WHO WORKED AT THE DAILY NEWSPAPER *THE CHICAGO TRIBUNE* TO WRITE A BLOG ASKING THEM TO DONATE A PENNY EACH TO HELP FUND HIS TUITION FEE. MONTHS LATER HE MANAGED TO GATHER THE EQUIVALENT OF 2.9 MILLION PENNIES. HE MANAGED GRADUATION FROM HIS DEGREE FOOD SCIENCE AND HAD HIS TUITION FEES ALL PAID FOR. *ASK AND YOU SHALL RECEIVE.*

HELL'S KITCHEN IS A VERY POPULAR CHEF FOOD PROGRAM WITH CELEBRITY CHEF GORDAN RAMSEY. AFTER FINISHING, THE CONTESTANTS ARE TAKEN FOR PSYCHIATRIC EVALUATION DUE TO THE INTENSITY OF THE SHOW. CONTESTANTS ARE ALSO GIVEN A MANICURE AND MASSAGES.

SUSANNA KLATTEN, THE RICHEST WOMAN IN GERMANY, USED A FAKE ALIAS WHILST WORKING IN AN INTERNSHIP FOR BMW. SHE WANTED TO BE SURE THAT WHEN SHE MET THE RIGHT PARTNER, HE WAS IN LOVE WITH HER FOR ALL THE RIGHT REASONS NOT JUST FOR HER MONEY. *I CAN'T SAY I BLAME HER.*

EINSTEIN WASN'T A CITIZEN OF ISRAEL. HOWEVER, HE WAS JEWISH. THE GERMAN-BORN PHYSICIST WAS OFFERED THE POST FOR THE PRESIDENT OF US, BUT TURNED IT DOWN.

A STUDY CONDUCTED IN 2011 SHOWS THAT THE BRAIN REACTS TO EMOTIONAL PAIN THE SAME WAY AS IT DOES PHYSICAL PAIN.

THE TERM JAYWALKER CAME FROM SLANG USED FOR PEOPLE WHO WERE SLOW OR SEEN AS STUPID. THEREFORE, WHEN SOMEONE IGNORE THE TRAFFIC LIGHT, THEY ARE CALLED A JAYWALKER. *I FEEL LIKE I'M A PRO JAYWALKER.*

THERE IS A HIDDEN BEACH IN ONE OF THE ISLANDS OF MEXICO WHICH WAS USED AS A BOMB TESTING SITE BY THE MEXICAN GOVERNMENT. IT WAS USED TO PREPARE FOR THE FIRST WORLD WAR.

IN *TOY STORY 3*, 'LOST THE BEAR' WAS ORIGINALLY MEANT TO BE IN THE FIRST MOVIE. HOWEVER, THE TECHNOLOGY REQUIRED TO MAKE HIS FUR WASN'T ADVANCED ENOUGH, SO IT GOT MOVED BACK.

SCIENTIST HAVE SHOWN THAT IT ONLY TAKES ABOUT 4 MINUTES OF YOU MEETING SOMEONE FOR YOU TO KNOW WHETHER YOU LIKE THEM OR NOT.

ONLY 3.6% OF PEOPLE WHO ARE OVER 65 ARE IN NURSING HOMES. ELDERLY MEN ARE LIKELY TO LIVE WITH A SPOUSE WHILE ELDERLY WOMEN ARE MORE LIKELY TO LIVE ALONE.

THERE ARE OVER 800 DIFFERENT LANGUAGES IN NEW YORK. THIS MAKES NEW YORK THE MOST LINGUISTICALLY DIVERSE CITY IN THE WORLD.

DURING THE TIME WILL SMITH WAS PLAYING THE FRESH PRINCE OF BEL-AIR HE WOULD FILE FOR BANKRUPTCY; HE OWED THE GOVERNMENT 2.8 MILLION DOLLARS. FOR THE FIRST THREE SEASONS OF THE SHOW WILL HAD TO PAY THE IRS 75% OF HIS EARNINGS.

BAMBOO IS THE FASTEST GROWING PLANT IN THE WORLD AND CAN EASILY GROW AS TALL AS 91 CENTIMETERS IN JUST ONE DAY.

THE CEOS OF SOUTHWEST AIRLINES AND STEVENS AVIATION SETTLED A DISPUTE OVER WHO WOULD HAVE THE SLOGAN 'PLANE SMART' BY HAVING A GOOD OLD-FASHIONED ARM WRESTLE. THEY WANTED TO AVOID GOING THROUGH A LONG LEGAL BATTLE. *IF ONLY POLITICAL QUARRELS COULD BE SETTLED THIS WAY.*

SO, YOU KNOW ABOUT RED TOMATOES, BUT HAVE YOU HEARD ABOUT BLACK TOMATOES? THEY ARE HEALTHY AND FULL OF AS ANTHOCYNANINS WHICH HELP WITH OBESITY, CANCER AND DIABETES.

TWO MUSLIMS HOLD THE KEY TO THE MOST SACRED SITE FOR CHRISTIANS, THE SITE WHERE JESUS WAS BELIEVED TO HAVE RISEN. THIS HAS BEEN TRADITION SINCE 1187.

IN CHINA, COAL WALKING IS A COMMON TRADITION. IF YOU'RE GETTING MARRIED, YOU HAVE TO CARRY THE BRIDE ON YOUR BACK ACROSS A PAN OF EXTREMELY HOT COALS BEFORE ENTERING YOUR NEW HOUSE. *I THINK I'D PASS ON THE BRIDE AND HOUSE, THANKS. I LIKE MY FEET.*

BACK IN THE 1918, THE COLOUR PINK WAS MARKETED AS BOY'S COLOUR, AND THE COLOUR BLUE WAS MARKETED AS A GIRL'S COLOUR. *HOW THINGS HAVE CHANGED.*

TO ENSURE RIDE OPERATORS WEREN'T RUSHING GUESTS, WALT DISNEY WENT TO HIS OWN THEME PARKS IN DISGUISES TO CHECK AND TEST IT.

ALTHOUGH PRAYING MANTISES ARE RELATIVELY SMALL, THEY ARE STILL ABLE TO CATCH AND EAT HUMMINGBIRDS.

SWITZERLAND HAS ENOUGH LEGAL SECTION SHELTERS TO ACCOMMODATION 11% OF ITS POPULATION.

IN SWITZERLAND IT IS ILLEGAL TO KEEP JUST ONE PIG BY ITSELF. THEY ARE VERY SOCIAL ANIMALS AND CAN BECOME VERY LONELY.

29% OF SAN FRANCISCO AIR POLLUTION COMES FROM CHINA. IT IS POSSIBLE FOR HAZARDOUS GASES TO TRAVEL IN THE AIR ACROSS SUCH FAR DISTANCES. THIS PROCESS DOESN'T TAKE LONG EITHER, JUST A COUPLE OF DAY IF THE WEATHER CONDITIONS ARE RIGHT.

ASTON KUTCHER IS AN AMERICA ACTOR WHO PLAYED JESSE IN THE BOX OFFICE HIT *DUDE, WHERE'S MY CAR?* HE THOUGHT ABOUT TAKING HIS OWN LIFE AT THE AGE OF 13 AS HE WANTED TO DONATE HIS OWN HEART TO HIS TWIN BROTHER MICHAEL, WHO SUFFERED FROM A HEART CONDITION.

HUMANS HAVE DIFFERENT ACCENTS, SO DO DUCKS. SCIENTIST HAVE SHOWN THE GEOGRAPHICAL LOCATION CAN AFFECT THE WAY A DUCK QUACKS.

A BULGARIAN MAN CALLED DOBRI DOBREV HAS WALKED OVER 25 KILOMETERS. HE WOULD DO THIS EVERY SINGLE DAY IN ORDER TO BEG FOR MONEY. HE WOULD THEN USE THIS MONEY TO HELP ORPHANAGES THAT COULDN'T PAY THEIR BILLS. IF HE WAS STILL ALIVE HE WOULD BE 106 YEARS OLD THIS YEAR.

WHEN YOU GET TICKLED AND START LAUGHING, THAT IS YOUR BODY'S DEFENCE MECHANISM. THIS IS NORMALLY A TRIGGER AS YOUR BODIES BEING SENT INTO A STATE OF PANIC AND ANXIETY.

LOMA LINDA UNIVERSITY SHOWED LAUGHER REALLY IS THE BEST MEDICINE, WITH STUDIES NOW SHOWING THAT LAUGHTER HELPS TO DECREASE THE NUMBER OF CANCER CELLS, AND BOOSTS THE IMMUNE SYSTEM. *I'VE LAUGHED SO MUCH DURING MY RESEARCH FOR THIS BOOK.*

THE MUSHROOMS IN *SUPER MARIO* ARE MAGIC MUSHROOMS WHICH HAVE THE PROPERTIES OF PSILOCYBIN, THE ACTIVE INGREDIENT THAT MAKES PEOPLE HALLUCINATE. THIS IS ALSO THE SAME THING MENTIONED IN *ALICE IN WONDERLAND.*

THERE IS A PENGUIN CALLED SIR NILES OLARVE, AN HONOURABLE MEMBER OF THE NORWEGIAN KING'S GUARD SINCE 1972. HE WAS OFFICIALLY KNIGHTED IN 2008. *NOTHING STRANGE AT ALL...*

THE BRILLIANT CUT IS THE MOST WELL-KNOWN CUT FOR A DIAMOND. THIS OCCURS WHEN A ROUND DIAMOND IS CUT PERFECTLY, SOMETHING KNOWN AS THE CUPID EFFECT WOULD APPEAR WHERE A LOVE HEART WOULD BE DISPLAYED. *SOUNDS LIKE A MARKETING STUNT TO ME.*

IN 2014 A HOMEOWNER IN ENGLAND ACCIDENTALLY FORGOT TO CLOSE HIS BEDROOM. HE LEFT THE HOUSE FOR THREE MONTHS. AFTER COMING BACK, HE DISCOVERED ROUGHLY 5,000 WASPS HAD SUNK IN AND BUILT A MASSIVE NEST IN THE BED.

GLADIATORS IN ROMAN TIMES WERE NOTHING LIKE WHAT YOU SEE IN THE MOVIES. THEY WERE MORE LIKE CELEBRITIES WHO WERE THERE TO PUT ON A GREAT SHOW, WITH MANY OF THE FIGHTS BEING CHOREOGRAPHED, SORT OF HOW PROFESSIONAL WRESTLING IS NOWADAYS.

EVEN THOUGH CHICAGO HAS ONE OF THE TOUGHEST GUN CONTROL SYSTEMS IN AMERICA, THE NUMBER OF PEOPLE WHO ARE MURDERED THERE IS DOUBLE THE NUMBER OF AMERICAN SOLDIERS WHO HAVE DIED IN AFGHANISTAN.

SOME BEARS IN RUSSIA ARE ADDICTED TO SNIFFING JET FUEL OUT OF DISCARDED BARRELS. IT GOT TO THE POINT WHERE THE BEARS WOULD STALK HELICOPTERS SO THEY CAN SNIFF THE DROPS OF FUELS LEFT BEHIND. *MUST BE A CRAZY HIGH.*

ONE MAN, TSUTOMU YAMAGUCHI, MANAGED TO SURVIVE BOTH ATOMIC BOMBINGS OF HIROSHIMA AND NAGASAKI. *I THINK WE'VE FOUND SUPER MAN.*

EACH YEAR ON JULY THE 4TH, AMERICANS ALL OVER THE NATION JOIN IN THE CELEBRATION OF INDEPENDENCE DAY. HOWEVER, THE REAL DATE FOR INDEPENDENCE IS JULY THE 22ND. THIS IS WHEN THE SECOND CONTINENTAL CONGRESS IN PHILADELPHIA VOTED TO APPROVE THE RESOLUTION.

THERE WAS A SOCIAL MOVEMENT HAPPENING IN THE EARLY 1960S CALLED THE TECHNOCRACY, WHICH INTENDED TO OVERRULE NORMAL GOVERNMENTS RUN BY POLITICIANS. THE TECHNOCRACY MOVEMENT PROPOSED TO HAVE SCIENTISTS TAKE OVER THE GOVERNMENT.

WHEN TWO LOVERS GAZE INTO EACH OTHER'S EYES, THEIR HEART BEATS SYNCHRONISE.

ABRAHAM LINCOLN WAS NOT ONLY 6 FOOT 4 BUT ALSO A VERY GOOD WRESTLER. HE ONLY LOST ONE OF HIS 300 CONTESTS. HE WOULD GO ONTO BECOME A COUNTY CHAMPION. *AND OF COURSE, WOULD BE THE PEOPLE'S CHAMP THEREAFTER.*

THE OLDEST PERSON EVER TO HAVE LIVED IS JEANNE CALMENT (FRENCH), WHO LIVED TO BE 122 YEARS AND 164 DAYS.

AUSTRALIAN MAN DON RICHIE LIVED NEAR A CLIFF CALLED THE GAP. THIS AREA HAS ONE OF THE HIGHEST RATES OF SUICIDE. RICHIE WAS ABLE TO SAVE OVER 160 LIVES BY PREVENTION OF SUICIDE. HE WOULD START UP A CONVERSATION WITH THEM AND OFFER THEM A CUP OF TEA. *WHAT A MAN.*

IF YOU WANTED TO GET A NEW SET OF TEETH IN 1815, IT WOULD HAVE BEEN FROM A DEAD SOLIDER'S MOUTH.

IN 2011 AMERICA, A THIRD OF DIVORCES FILED WERE FOUND TO CONTAIN THE WORD 'FACEBOOK'.

NATIONAL GEOGRAPHIC STAR CASEY ANDERSON HAS A PET GRIZZLY BEAR CALLED BRUTUS. WHEN BRUTUS WAS BORN, HE WAS ADOPTED AND WOULD GO ON TO SERVE AS CASEY'S BEST MAN. *WHY CAN'T I HAVE A RELATIONSHIP LIKE THIS?*

ALBERT EINSTEIN'S BRAIN WAS KEPT AND TAKEN APART AGAINST HIS WISHES.

TIMOTHY LEARY WAS AN AMERICAN PSYCHOLOGIST AND WRITER WHO WAS A STRONG ADVOCATE FOR PSYCHEDELICS. HE WAS SENT TO JAIL IN 1970. HE COMPLETED A SERIES OF TESTS TO DECIDE WHICH PRISON HE WOULD BE SENT TO. 8 MONTHS INTO HIS SENTENCE HE WOULD ESCAPE. ANDERSON CREATED THE TEST HIMSELF AND MANAGED TO MANIPULATE THE RESULTS, SO HE GOT SENTENCED AS A GARDENER IN A LOW SECURITY PRISON.

RESEARCH HAS PROVIDED EVIDENCE THAT INTENSE, TRAUMATIZING EVENTS SUCH AS A BREAK-UPS, DIVORCES, LOSS OF LOVED ONES, PHYSICAL SEPARATION FROM A LOVED ONE OR BETRAYAL CAN CAUSE REAL PHYSICAL PAINS IN THE AREA OF ONE'S HEART.

IN KANSAS THERE'S A CITY CALLED GAS, DUE TO THE ABSURD AMOUNT OF GAS FOUND AROUND IN THE AREA.

IN YOAKHAR, OLD RUSSIA, THERE IS A SCHOOL CALLED ORDINARY MIRACLE AND IT LOOKS IDENTICAL TO A CASTLE. THE DESIGNER OF THIS BUILDING HAD A WIFE, SO HE THOUGHT TO BUILD A SCHOOL WHICH KIDS WOULD WANT TO GO TO. *WOULDN'T THAT BE EXCITING.*

DID YOU KNOW THAT BARCODE SCANNERS SCAN THE WHITE SPACES RATHER THAN THE BLACK?

WHEN RETURNING TO EARTH, THE *APOLLO 11* CREW HAD TO QUARANTINE IN A SPECIAL FACULTY FOR THREE WEEKS AS IT WAS UNKNOWN WHETHER THEY'D BROUGHT BACK ANY GERMS WITH THEM.

THE WORLD'S MOST EXPENSIVE LICENSE PLATE WAS PURCHASED BY A YOUNG BUSINESSMAN CALLED SAEED ABDUL GHAFOOR KHOURI. THE PLATE COST HIM 14.3 MILLION DOLLARS. AND HAS THE LATE ONE. *14.3 SOUNDS LIKE A RIP OFF TO ME.*

IN THE MAHARASHTRA STATE OF INDIA, THERE IS SOMETHING DONE WHICH IS CALLED BABY TOSSING. COULD YOU HAVE A GUESS WHAT IT CONSISTS OF? THAT'S RIGHT TOSSING BABIES...THEY BELIEVE THAT BRINGS THE CHILDREN GOOD LUCK, A LONG HEALTHY LIFE AND LOTS OF INTELLIGENCE. *BEING TOSSED AS A BABY CLEARLY GIVES THEM THE INTELLIGENCE TO TOSS THEIR BABIES.*

WE ALL LOVE OUR PARACETAMOL AND IBUPROFEN BUT DITCH THAT, HAVE YOU TRIED USING KETCHUP? IN THE 1830S, KETCHUP WAS SOLD AND MARKETED AS A CURE FOR INDIGESTION BY AN OHIO PHYSICIAN NAMED JOHN COOK.

THE GREATEST PIRATE OF ALL TIME WAS
ACTUALLY A CHINESE WOMAN CALLED
CHING SHIH. SHE WAS ORIGINALLY A
PROSTITUTE WHO MARRIED A RED FLAG
FLEET COMMANDER WHO AT THAT TIME,
CONTROLLED THE SOUTH CHINA SEAS. HE
SAW HER AS AN EQUAL. SHE WOULD GO ON
TO PROVE AND EARN THE RESPECT OF THE
CREW MEMBERS. DURING HER TIME AS
CAPTAIN SHE ACCUMULATED OVER 300
WARSHIPS, WITH OVER 1,200 SUPPORTS
SHIPS AND CLOSE TO 80,000 PIRATES
FOLLOWING HER. *NOW THAT'S A BAD B.*

WHEN DOCTORS HAD TO WORK ON
VIOLINIST ROGER FRISCH'S BRAIN
OPERATION, THERE WAS A PRIVATE
CONCERT. HE HAD TO BE AWAKE WHEN
THE SURGERY WAS TAKING PLACE AND
PLAYED THE VIOLIN TO EASE AND RELAX
HIMSELF.

THE LEANING TOWER OF PISA BEGAN TO LEAN DURING CONSTRUCTION IN THE 12TH CENTURY, DUE TO SOFT GROUND WHICH COULD NOT PROPERLY SUPPORT THE STRUCTURE'S WEIGHT. IT WORSENED THROUGH THE COMPLETION OF CONSTRUCTION IN THE 14TH CENTURY. BY 1990, THE TILT HAD REACHED 5.5 DEGREES.

THE ANCIENT ROMANS OFTEN DRANK STALE URINE AS MOUTHWASH. *THAT'S NASTY.*

APPLE MANAGED TO GENERATE 43.7 BILLION DOLLARS IN SALES WITHIN THE FIRST QUARTER OF 2014.

SINCE 2005, THERE HAS NOT BEEN A SINGLE HUMAN WHO HAS WON A GAME OF CHESS AGAINST A HIGH-TECH COMPUTER. THIS IS UNLIKELY TO CHANGE SINCE COMPUTERS ARE INCREASINGLY POWERFUL.

CAN YOU GUESS THE REASON WHY
MONOPOLY WAS INVENTED? MONOPOLY
WAS INVENTED IN 1903. THE COMPANY
WANTED TO EXPOSE JUST HOW UNFAIR THE
SOCIAL SYSTEM IS. THE GAME REPLICATES
HOW A SMALL MINORITY TAKING A LARGE
PORTION OF THE MONEY AND THE LARGE
MAJORITY TAKING LESS OF THE MONEY.

A MESSAGE FROM ME TO YOU!

I hope you've enjoyed reading this book as much as I have enjoyed writing it. I am planning to make this into a series of books so if you have enjoyed it, make sure to go and leave a review/rating on the Amazon store, it helps me out more than you can imagine and by that, I mean it creates social proof for this book which means more money in my pockets. Who knows, I might even reinvest and add illustrations. But no seriously, thank you for purchasing this book. I hope it's been insightful and random enough for you.

On a more personal level, I just want to let you know that no matter where you find yourself in life, no matter how good or bad the situation, always take the time to reflect and understand that you are in full control of your life and your reality. Life will always challenge you, it's just the yin and yang. It's a strange but beautiful way to grow as a character!

Always choose to love, not hate. Always choose to laugh, not cry. I'm wishing you an amazing rest of your life filled with love, happiness and great fortune.

REFERENCES

Bakolli, V., 2020. *17 Truly Odd Historical Facts That I Had A Hard Time Believing Were Real*. [online] Buzz-Feed. Available at: <https://www.buzzfeed.com/valez-abakolli/wild-historical-facts-that-are-actually-true> [Accessed 23 November 2020].

Bambora. n.d. *Why The Nordics Are Going Cashless*. [online] Available at: <https://www.bambora.com/ar-ticles/why-the-nordics-are-going-cashless/> [Accessed 1 December 2020].

Brown, M., n.d. *Fact Check: It's True, U.S. Government Poisoned Some Alcohol During Prohibition*. [online] Eu.us-atoday.com. Available at: <https://eu.usatoday.-com/story/news/factcheck/2020/06/30/fact-check-u-s-government-poisoned-some-alcohol-during-prohibition/3283701001/> [Accessed 4 December 2020].

Cooper, K., 2019. *Rights To Light Misunderstandings | Party Wall Law | Morrisons Solicitors*. [online] Morrlaw. Available at: <https://www.morrlaw.com/party-

wall/rights-to-light-misunderstandings/> [Accessed 4 December 2020].

Daniel, A., 2013. *50 Amazing Historical Facts You Never Knew | Best Life*. [online] Best Life. Available at: <https://bestlifeonline.com/historical-facts/> [Accessed 1 December 2020].

Facts, R., n.d. *9,913 Random Facts You Didn't Know ← Factslides →*. [online] Factslides.com. Available at: <http://factslides.com/> [Accessed 4 December 2020].

H., 2018. *Here Are Some Of The Strangest Phobias One Can Have - Ergophobia*. [online] The Economic Times. Available at: <https://economictimes.indiatimes.com/industry/miscellaneous/here-are-some-of-the-strangest-phobias-one-can-have/ergopho-bia/slideshow/64338219.cms> [Accessed 25 November 2020].

Hellmann, M., 2021. *Dubai to Build World's First Temperature-Controlled Indoor 'City'*. [online] Time. Available at: <https://time.com/2964797/dubai-to-build-worlds-first-temperature-controlled-indoor-city/> [Accessed 2 February 2021].

HISTORY. 2019. *10 Things You Didn'T Know About William Shakespeare*. [online] Available at: <https://www.history.com/news/10-things-you-

didnt-know-about-william-shakespeare> [Accessed 27 November 2020].

Howard, B., 2020. *Why Did L.A. Drop 96 Million 'Shade Balls' Into Its Water?*. [online] National Geographic. Available at: <https://www.nationalgeographic.com/news/2015/08/150812-shade-balls-los-angeles-California-drought-water-environment/> [Accessed 1 December 2020].

Jay, C., 2016. *Organ Transplants: A Change Of Heart In More Ways Than One? – Scientific Scribbles*. [online] Blogs.unimelb.edu.au. Available at: https://blogs.unimelb.edu.au/sciencecommunication/2016/10/15/

Lanzendorfer, J., 2016. *10 Fascinating Facts About Ravens*. [online] Mentalfloss.com. Available at: https://www.mentalfloss.com/article/53295/10-fascinating-facts-about-ravens

McGrath, M., 2013. *Dolphins Have 'Longest Social Memory' Among Non-Humans*. [online] BBC News. Available at: <https://www.bbc.co.uk/news/science-environment-23589041> [Accessed 31 November 2020].

OMGFacts. 2020. *Omgfacts Home*. [online] Available at: <http://omgfacts.com/> [Accessed 1 December 2020].

Reddit.com. n.d. *Today I Learned (TIL)*. [online] Available at: <https://www.reddit.com/r/todayilearned/> [Accessed 4 December 2020].

Reilly, L., 2018. *Signalman Jack: The Baboon Who Worked For The Railroad—And Never Made A Mistake*. [online] Mentalfloss.com. Available at: <https://www.mentalfloss.com/article/559031/signalman-jack-baboon-worked-railroad-south-africa#:~:text=One%20-day%20in%20the%201880s,his%20pet%20and%20per-sonal%20assistant> [Accessed 1 November 2020].

Reynolds, E., 2012. *Teenager Collapses And Dies After Playing Online Computer Game For 40 HOURS Straight*. [online] Mail Online. Available at: <https://www.dailymail.co.uk/news/article-2175410/Teenager-dies-playing-game-40-HOURS-straight-eating.html> [Accessed 2 December 2020].

Ryan, S., 2014. *How Is Silk Made? And Is It Humane?*. [online] Greenopedia. Available at: <https://greenopedia.com/wild-peace-silk/> [Accessed 10 November 2020].

Sample, I., 2010. *The Price Of Love? Losing Two Of Your Closest Friends*. [online] The Guardian. Available at: https://www.theguardian.com/science/2010/sep/15/price-love-close-friends-relationship

Society, N., n.d. Honey Ant Adaptations. [online] National Geographic Society. Available at: <https://www.nationalgeographic.org/media/honey-ant-adaptations-wbt/> [Accessed 29 November 2020].

The Fact Site. 2020. *The Fact Site | Fun & Interesting Facts*. [online] Available at: <https://www.thefactsite.com/> [Accessed 1 December 2020].

Tikkanen, A., n.d. *Pablo Escobar: 8 Interesting Facts About The King Of Cocaine*. [online] Encyclopedia Britannica. Available at: <https://www.britannica.com/list/pablo-escobar-8-interesting-facts-about-the-king-of-cocaine> [Accessed 1 December 2020].

Jones, L., 2011. *LIZ JONES: As A Tennis Star Admits Reducing Her Bust To Improve Her Game... Breast Reduction Boosted My Career But Didn't Bring Me Happiness*. [online] Mail Online. Available at: <https://www.dailymail.co.uk/femail/article-2008894/Breast-reduction-boosted-career-didnt-bring-happiness.html> [Accessed 19 November 2020].

WTF Fun Facts. 2020. *WTF Fun Facts - Funny, Interesting, And Weird Facts*. [online] Available at: <https://wtf-funfact.com/> [Accessed 4 December 2020].

Made in the USA
Coppell, TX
19 February 2022

73790424R10057